Prayers That Availeth Much"

LaRose Angela Richardson

REJOICE
Essential Publishing

Prayers That Availeth Much/ LaRose Angela Richardson

ISBN-13: 978-1-952312-15-1

Library of Congress Control Number: 2020908055

Table of Contents

Foreword

"*Prayers That Availeth Much*," is something that LaRose Angela Richardson walks in. I have had the privilege of watching her faith in action. When she believed God for healing, she spoke the Word, and it manifested. When she heard how God moved in someone's life for their healing, she knew that if God did it for them, then He would duplicate it in her life. Her hunger for God allows His power to move in her. Once the Lord grew her leg out without the doctors performing surgery. When LaRose heard about people's credit score going up supernaturally through our prayer line, she said, "I'm Next!" Shortly afterward, her score increased several points. LaRose is serious about prayer. She wakes up at 6 a.m. throughout the week and prays in her heavenly language for an hour. Additionally, she prays again with our prayer team at noon. You will quickly realize the gift of exhortation on her life as you read the pages in this book. Your faith will increase for God to do the miraculous in your life as LaRose shares her testimonies. You will be inspired to apply the revelation that she gives. She knows how to get prayer to the throne room. Why not learn from someone who practices what they preach? "*Prayers That Availeth Much*," is a powerful tool that intercessors need. LaRose exposes many demonic strongholds that the average person may not be aware of, and she provides declarations and prayers to set the captives free. LaRose will show you how to keep your deliverance. I highly recommend praying these prayers repeatedly for your breakthrough. Get ready to go to your next level in God!

Author Kimberly Moses
Founder of Rejoice Essential Magazine and Publishing

Acknowledgments

I like to thank God for giving me the ability to write this book, *"Prayers that Availeth Much,"* because when we pray and obey God, then our prayers will be answered.

I like to thank Prophetess Kimberly Moses for being obedient to God by having a continuous mentorship program to help get me to the next level in the Lord. She is an answer to prayer. I prayed and asked God to send me someone to teach, coach, and help me be all that I can be in Him. Through her mentorship, she has spoken life into me, which has helped me step out of my comfort zone from behind the scenes to move into greater things in God.

I would like to thank my husband, Richard Richardson, who has stood by my side from day one and encouraged me to do more things with my writing. He has coached me in doing videos to post on Facebook and other social media sites. I thank him for the prayers and the encouragement that he has given me now and over the years.

I would like to thank my Apostle Troy Williams & Pastor Carmella Williams for all their encouragement to keep moving in the things of God. Also, to Pastor Louella Jackson for her motivation and her boost to do teaching from my book "Walking In Total Freedom After Healing From Deep Inner Wounds" and for starting a book club.

God, I thank You for the covenant people that You have placed in my life to help push me to the next level in You.

Introduction

Prayer is very important in the life of a believer. According to Merriam-Webster, prayer means a solemn request for help or expression of thanks addressed to God.[1] The Greek word for prayer is "proseuchomai," which means to pray to God; supplicate; worship; pray; make prayer.[2] Prayers that are rooted in Scriptures are guaranteed to be aligned with the heart of

1. Prayer" Merriam-Webster.com 2019, https://www.Merriam-Webster.com accessed 09-23-20191

2. Greek word for prayer "proseuchoamia" https://www.biblehub.com accessed 09-23-2019

God. When we pray the Scriptures back to Him, He is obligated to answer His Word. We are to pray like Daniel prayed. He prayed three times a day, regardless of the sanctions that were placed on him by King Nebuchadnezzar. He refused to let anyone tell him when he could pray and to whom those prayers were offered. Daniel knew the One and only true God, Abba Father. There are three in the Trinity: God the Father, God the Son, and God the Holy Ghost. There will never be any other deity that has the Sovereignty that the Trinity possesses. They are All Powerful. In Daniel 10, Daniel prayed for 21 days without getting an answer and he received a visit from an angel, who explained why it took so long to get his prayers answered. Daniel was very persistent with his prayers. He didn't give up on the fifth day because his prayers weren't answered, but he continued to offer supplication to God. When we continue to pray over the matter instead of quitting, it shows great faith to believe that God is going to do what He has promised us.

Then said he to me, "Do not be afraid, Daniel, for from the first day that you set your heart on understanding this and on humbling yourself before God, your words were heard, and I have come in response to your words." — Daniel 10:12 (AMP)

Daniel's prayers were delayed because the King of Persia (demonic spirit) in the Second Heaven kept the angel from passing through to get the answer to him. As a response to his prayers, the angel came and told Daniel not to be afraid because from the first day that he purposed to understand and humbled himself before God, his words were heard.

The King of Persia had fought the angel for 21 days, then Michael, one of the Chief Princes came to help him get through to the third heaven to bring the answer to Daniel. So just like Daniel prayed, we must as well no matter how long it takes for us to receive an answer. Many times, we may not get immediate manifestations, but that shouldn't be a deterrent. If we keep praying, we will have prayers that "Availeth Much." We are too close to give up now. Our answer could be just around the corner. Some of my family members need to know God because, at this point, if they were to die, they would spend eternity in a devil's hell. So, I know that I can't give up on them now because they are closer to salvation than when I first started praying for them.

Here are some potent prayers to pray that 'Available Much' and God will send the angels with our answers. When we humble ourselves before God like Daniel did, then we can have answers to our prayers as well. Do you know that some of our prayers are keeping people alive? How? Because we are interceding for them and asking God to let them live until they give their lives to Jesus. Our prayers are more powerful than we think. Don't stop interceding for your families, children, marriages, our nation and President, and so on.

"Therefore, confess your sins to one another (your false steps, your offenses), and pray for one another, that you may be healed and restored. The heartfelt and persistent prayer of a righteous man(believer) can accomplish much (when out into action and made effective by God) --it is dynamic and can have tremendous power." — James 5:16 (AMP)

Let's enter the Holy of Holies because we need to abide in the Secret Place where God dwells. Here are some prayers that will take you there.

CHAPTER ONE

Healing

Healing is the process of making or becoming sound or healthy (Merriam-Webster).[3] In Greek, the word healing is "iama," which means healing, curing, remedy.[4] Throughout the Bible, Jesus healed many who were oppressed with spirits, illnesses or diseases. We are to pray the Scriptures back to God because He is only obligated to answer His Word. James 5: 14-15 (AMP) says, "Is anyone among you sick? He must call for the

3. "healing" Merriam-Webster 2019, https://www.Merriam-Webster.com accessed 09-23-2019
4. Greek word for healing "iama" https://www.biblehub.com accessed 09-23-2019

elders (spiritual leaders) of the church and they are to pray over him, anointing him with oil in the name of the Lord; "And the prayers of the faith will restore the one who is sick, and the Lord will raise him up; and if he has committed sin, he will be forgiven."

One of the things that we must remember is that God wants to heal us from our infirmities, illnesses, and sickness. Many times, people have been healed by just declaring healing Scriptures daily. They spoke the Word of God until it permeated their hearts, then they began to walk as if they were already healed. This practice of declaring has built up their faith to the next level in God. Declarations can be made personal when we add our name to some of the Scriptures. There are so many promises in the Bible about healing. God is ready to honor His word and heal all your sicknesses, mental issues, and diseases.

DECLARATIONS

Heal me, Oh Lord, and I will be healed. (Jeremiah 17:14 AMP)

I will call on the elders of the church to pray over me and anoint me with oil in the name of the Lord. (James 5:14)

Worship the Lord your God, and His blessings will be on your food and water. (Exodus 23:25)

I do not have to fear for you are with me, God. (Isaiah 41:10)

Lord, you will strengthen me and help me and uphold me with Your righteous right hand. (Isaiah 41:10)

Jesus took all our pain and bore all of our sicknesses. (Isaiah 53:4)

By His stripes, we are healed. (Isaiah 53:5)

"For I will restore health to you and heal you of your wounds," says the Lord. (Jeremiah 30:17 AMP)

Dear friend, I pray that you may enjoy good health and that all may go well with you, even as your soul is getting along well." (3 John 2 NIV)

"And my God will meet all your needs according to the riches of his glory in Christ Jesus." (Philippians 4:19 NIV)

PRAYER

Father God, in the name of Jesus, I come before You today to ask that You touch the person that is reading this prayer right now. Lord, You said in Your Word that by Your stripes, we are healed. Lord, I declare Psalms 30:2 (NIV) over them, "Lord my God, I called to you for help, and you healed me." I speak healing from the top of their heads to the soles of their feet right now in Jesus' name. Lord, You said in Jeremiah 30:17 (NIV), "But I will restore you to health and heal your wounds," declares the Lord. Satan, the blood of Jesus is against you. Get out of their bodies because you have no legal right to attack them with illnesses or diseases! Lord, You said in Matthew 9:35 (NIV) that Jesus went through all the towns and villages, teaching in their synagogues, proclaiming the good news of the Kingdom, and healing every disease and sickness. I command all symptoms to be null and void right now. Go back to the abyss in Jesus' name. Lord, You are Jehovah Rapha, the God that healeth thee. Lord, send Your healing virtue to saturate them in any area of their bodies so they can walk out in their healing. Lord, we cancel and veto the spirit of infirmity, inflammation, and infection right now in Jesus' name. We command it to go back to the abyss from where it came in Jesus' name.

We command the spirit of arthritis and any type of bone pain, cancer, diabetes, high blood pressure, hormonal issues, stomach disorders to cease right now in Jesus' name. Lord, You said in Your word that "A cheerful heart is good medicine, but a crushed spirit dries up the bones." Lord, send Your peace that passeth all understanding to guard their hearts and minds in

Christ Jesus. Lord, we are thanking You in advance for the healing that will hit their bodies and their lives right now in Jesus' name. Lord, we give You all the glory, honor, and praise right now in Jesus' name. Amen.

CHAPTER TWO

Mental Illness

According to the Mayo Clinic, mental illnesses are also called mental health disorders, which refers to a wide range of mental conditions. Some disorders affect your mood, thinking, and behavior. Some examples of mental illnesses are depression, anxiety disorders, eating disorders, and addictive behaviors, OCD, and many other diseases in this class.[5] The definition of lunatic by Merriam-Webster is a mentally ill

5. Mayoclinic.org, mental illness https:// www.mayoclinic.org accessed 09-23-2019

person, madman.[6] The Greek word for Lunatic is "seleniazetai," an epileptic or "moonstruck."[7] Matthew 17:15 says, "Lord have mercy on my son: for he is lunatick, and sore vexed; for often times he falleth into the fire, and oft into the water." When disorders start to affect your normal daily activities, it is time to seek deliverance or medical help. Some people have an anxiety disorder where they are scared to go around a group of people at one time, which is not normal. They may have to go on medication to prevent panic attacks. Deliverance is needed to overcome these disorders because they are demonic and come from the enemy.

Satan wants to stop you from reaching your God-given destiny. But with much prayer, fasting, and deliverance, all of these can be broken off your life so you can walk in total freedom in Christ Jesus. On the 'Get Bible' website, there is an article called the "Hope for Mental Illness," written in August 2015. It states that in one of every five adults, out of 60 million Americans will

6. "lunatic" Merriam-Webster 2019, https://www.Merrian-Webster. com accessed 09-23-2019
7. Greek word for lunatic "seleniazetai" https://www.biblehub.com accessed 09-23-2019

experience a mental illness in the coming year. This means that everyone of us knows someone who is living with a mental illness.

1. Half of all adults will have a mental illness in their lifetime.
2. Half of all chronic mental illnesses begin by the age of 14.
3. One of five children will have a mental illness by age 18.
4. Ninety percent of people who die by suicide also had mental illness[8]

DECLARATIONS

When the righteous cry for help, the Lord hears and delivers them out of all their troubles. (Psalm 34:17 ESV)

The Lord is near to the brokenhearted and saves the crushed in spirit (contrite in heart, truly sorry for their sin). (Psalm 34:18 AMP)

8. www.get-bible.com mental illness article accessed 09-23-2019

Many hardships and perplexing circumstances confront the righteous, But the Lord rescues him from them all. (Psalm 34:29 AMP)

Fear not, for I am with you; be not dismayed, for I am your God. (Isaiah 41:10 ESV)

I will strengthen you; I will help you; I will uphold you in my righteous right hand. (Isaiah 41:10 ESV)

For God gave us a spirit not of fear but of power and love and self-control. (2 Timothy 1:7 ESV)

PRAYER

Father God, in the name of Jesus, we come before You today to pray for the one that is reading this prayer right now. Lord, heal them spiritually, mentally, physically, and emotionally right now in Jesus' name. Lord, go deep down within their souls. Heal every broken place and wounded area in their hearts. Lord, You said in Your Word that You will supply our every need according to your riches in glory by Christ Jesus. So, Lord, they need You right now to heal and make them whole in Jesus' name. Lord, give them hope in a world where there seems to be none. We speak life into them right now in Jesus' name. Lord, let them know that they can find supernatural hope in you, Jesus. Lord, let them know that You love them and care about everything that concerns them in Jesus' name. Lord, let your healing virtue saturate their hearts. Remove their hardened heart and give them a heart of flesh in Jesus' name. Lord, heal every wound in their souls so they can live a long and peaceful life in Jesus' name. I speak joy in their lives. Lord, You said that the joy of the Lord is our strength. Strengthen them right now in Jesus' name. Lord, let the peace that passeth all understanding guard their hearts and minds in Christ Jesus. Lord, we thank You for their total healing right now in Jesus' name. Amen.

CHAPTER THREE

Forgiveness

Forgiveness is the action or process of forgiving or being forgiven.[9] The Greek word for forgiveness is "aphiemi," which is to leave someone or something alone, to send away, complete forgiveness.[10] In the Lord's prayer, we pray for God to forgive us of our trespasses as we forgive those who trespass against us. When we forgive, we are not letting the offender off the hook, but it is

---

9. "forgiveness" Merriam-Webster.com 2019, https://www.
Merriam-Webster.com accessed 09-23-2019
10. Greek word for forgiveness "aphiemi" https://www.biblehub.
com accessed 09-23-2019

helping us to move forward in the things of God. When we walk in unforgiveness, there is a wall between God and us because of the offense that we insist on carrying instead of releasing it. If we are having a hard time forgiving people, then we need to pray and ask God to help us forgive the person who has hurt us. We need to be real with God and let Him know exactly where we are in this process. We can ask God for an extra dose of grace to be able to forgive the offender. We can activate grace through our faith. Grace is more than unmerited favor, but it is the ability to do what we can't do on our own. Paul talked about it in 2 Corinthians 12 when he asked God to remove a hindrance that he was dealing with three times.

God told Paul in 2 Corinthians 12:9 (ESV), "My grace is sufficient for you, for my power is made perfect in weakness." God's power is greatest when we are at our weakest. The Word states, "Let the weak say I am strong." We are stronger in God than we are in our own strength. With God's supernatural strength, we can do anything but fail. So, we shouldn't have any issues walking in forgiveness because God has forgiven us of our past, present, and future sins. So, we can forgive other people for their trespasses against us.

DECLARATIONS

Bearing one another and, if one has a complaint against another forgiving each other; as the Lord has forgiven you, so you also must forgive. (Colossians 3:13 ESV)

And forgive us our debts, as we also have forgiven our debtors. (Matthew 6:12 ESV)

So, watch yourselves. "If your brother or sister sins against you, rebuke them; and if they repent, forgive them. (Luke 17:3 NIV)

Even if they sin against you seven times in a day and seven times comes back to you saying, "I repent," you must forgive them. (Luke 17:4 NIV)

Get rid of all bitterness, rage, and anger, brawling and slander, along with every form of malice. (Ephesians 4:31 NIV)

Be kind and compassionate to one another, forgiving each other, just as Christ God forgave you. (Ephesians 4:32 NIV)

If we confess our sins, he is faithful and just and will forgive us our sins and purify us from all unrighteousness. (1 John 1:9 NIV)

Repent, then, and turn to God, so that your sins may be wiped out. (Acts 3:19 NIV)

Therefore, if anyone is in Christ, the new creation has come: The old has gone, the new is here! (2 Corinthians 5:17 NIV)

In him, we have redemption through his blood, the forgiveness of sins, in accordance with the riches of God's grace. (Ephesians 1:7 NIV)

PRAYER

Father God, in the name of Jesus, I come before You today to ask that You help me to walk in forgiveness with everyone that has mistreated me throughout the years until this present time. Lord, give me a pure heart and clean hands so I won't run to mischief in Jesus' name. Lord, renew a right spirit within me and make me whiter than snow. Lord, help me to walk in your agape love right now with everyone that I may meet from this day forward in Jesus' name. Lord, let my life be illuminated with your presence in Jesus' name. Lord, thank You for forgiving me of my past, present, and future sins over 2,000 years ago when You put everything on Jesus on the cross. I can now walk in the freedom that You promised me in Your Word. Lord, go deep into my heart and soul. Remove anything that is not like You from my life right now in Jesus' name. Lord, I thank You for making all things new in my life from this day forth in Jesus' name. Lord, I thank You for perfecting me with Your love in Jesus' name. Amen.

PSALM 91 PRAYER OF PROTECTION (AMP)

1. He who dwells in the shelter of the Most High Will remain secure and rest in the shadow of the Almighty (whose power no enemy can withstand).

2. I will say of the Lord, "He is my refuge and my fortress, My God, in whom I trust (with great confidence, and on whom I rely)"

3. For He will save you from the trap of the fowler, And from the deadly pestilence.

4. He will cover you and completely protect you with His pinions, And under His wings, you will find refuge, His faithfulness is a shield and a wall.

5. You will not be afraid of the terror of night, Nor of the arrow that flies by day,

6. Nor of the pestilence that stalks in darkness, Nor of the destruction (sudden death) that lays waste at noon,

7. A thousand may fall at your side And ten thousand at your right hand, But danger will not come near you.

8. You will only (be a spectator as you) look on with your eyes And witness the (divine) repayment of the wicked (as watch safely from the shelter of the Most High.

9. Because you have made the Lord, (who is) my refuge, Even the Most High, your dwelling place.

10. No evil will befall you, Nor will any plague come near your tent.

11. Nor He will command His angels in regard to you, To protect and defend and guard you in all your ways (of obedience and service).

12. They will lift you up in their hands, So that you do not (even) strike your foot against a stone.

13. You will tread upon the lion and cobra; The young lion and the serpent you will trample underfoot.

14. Because he set his love on Me, therefore I will save him; I will set him (securely) on high because he knows My name (he confidently trusts and relies on Me, knowing I will never abandon him no, never)

15. He will call upon Me, and I will answer him, I will be with him in trouble, I will rescue him and honor him.

16. With a long life, I will satisfy him And I will let him see My salvation.

PRAYER OF JABEZ (AMP)

1 Chronicles 4: 9-10

9. Jabez was more honorable than his brothers, but his mother named him Jabez saying, "Because I gave birth to him in pain." 10, Jabez cried out to the God of Israel, saying, "Oh, that You would indeed bless me and enlarge my border (property), and Your hand would be with me, and You would keep me from evil so that it does not hurt me!" And God granted his request.

PSALM 23 (AMP)

1. The Lord is my Shepherd (to feed, to guide, and to shield me), I shall not want.

2. He lets me lie down in green pastures; He leads me beside the still and quiet waters.

3. He refreshes and restores my soul (life); He leads me in the paths of righteousness for His name's sake.

4. Even though I walk through the (sunless) valley of the shadow of death, O guide, they

comfort and console me. I fear no evil, for You are with me; Your rod (to protect) and Your staff.

5. You prepare a table before me in the presence of my enemies. You have anointed and refreshed my head with oil; My cup overflows.

6. Surely goodness and mercy and unfailing love shall follow me all the days of my life, And I shall dwell forever (throughout all my days) in the house and in the presence of the Lord.

LORD'S PRAYER (AMP)

Matthew 6:9-13

9. Pray, then, in this way Our Father, who is in heaven, Hallowed be Your Name.

10. Your kingdom come. Your will be done on earth as it is in heaven.

11. Give us this day our daily bread.

12. and forgive us our debts, as we have forgiven our debtors (letting go of both the wrong and the resentment).

13. and do not lead us into temptation but deliver us from evil.

14. (For Yours is the kingdom and the power and the glory forever. Amen)

CHAPTER FOUR

Patience

Merriam-Webster defines patience as the capacity to accept or tolerate delay, trouble, or suffering without getting angry or upset.[11] The Greek word for patience is "hupomone," which is endurance, steadfastness, or patient for waiting.[12] God wants us to have the patience of Job. Even in our walk with Him, things may not happen suddenly. Many times, we have to wait a while for even our prayers to come to fruition, but we

11. "patience" Merriam-Webster 2019, https://www.Merriam-Webste.com accessed 09-23-2019
12. Greek word for patience "hupomone" https://www.biblehub.com accessed 09-23-2019

must not get weary in well-doing. We must not give up because in this life, we are going to have trials and tribulations, but we can always go to God to help us make it through them. God will give us some of His supernatural strength to make it through our troubled times. We must stay on our faces before God and cry out to Him to help us make it through the storms. When we have prayed for a family member to get saved and it seems like it is a long time coming, we must not give up on them. God is working in the background, setting things in order for the appointed time of their salvation. Also, while we are waiting for our prophecies to manifest, we can be preparing for the promotion by taking some classes, reading books on the subject, praying, fasting, studying the Word of God and getting it down inside of our hearts. Ephesian 4:2 (NIV) says, "Be completely humble and gentle, be patient, bearing with one another in love."

DECLARATIONS (NIV)

Love is patient. Love is kind. It does not envy. It does not boast. It is good. (1 Corinthians 13:4)

Do not be anxious about anything, but in every situation by prayer and petition, with thanksgiving. (Philippians 4:6)

Present your requests to God. (Philippians 4:6)

A hot-tempered person stirs up conflict, but the one who is patient calms a quarrel. (Proverbs 15:18)

For I know the plans that I have for you, declares the Lord, plans to prosper you and not to harm you, plans to give you hope and a future. (Jeremiah 29:11)

Be joyful in hope, patient in affliction, faithful in prayer. (Romans 12:12)

You say, I choose the appointed time; it is I who judge with equity. (Psalm 75:2)

Let us not become weary in doing good, for at the proper time we will reap a harvest if we do not give up. (Galatians 6:9)

Be completely humble and gentle; be patient, bearing one another with love. (Ephesians 4:2)

PRAYER

Lord, help me to be more patient and understanding with people that are around me regularly. Also, help me to be more loving toward them in Jesus' name. Lord, help me to show your agape love wherever I go and with whoever I meet. Help me to give them a word in love and open their hearts to receive the Word of God. Help me not to get angry or frustrated when things don't go the way that I think it should. Lord, help me to be able to wait when You tell me, "No. Not yet," in Jesus' name. Lord, help me to change my attitude and walk in humility in Jesus' name. Lord, help me to remember that it is not about me, but it is about what You want to accomplish for my life. Lord, I give You permission to come inside of me and make all dead things new in Jesus' name. Lord, let Your supernatural endurance and patience live inside of my heart, mind, and soul in Jesus' name. Lord, uproot anything in my life that is not of you, Jesus. Lord, I give You my life so you can use me as You see fit. Lord, help me to die to myself so that I can move on in the Kingdom of God in Jesus' name. Lord, I praise you now for all You have done up until now in my life in Jesus' name. Amen.

CHAPTER FIVE

Fear

Merriam-Webster defines fear as an unpleasant emotion caused by the belief that someone or something is dangerous, likely to cause pain, threat.[13] The Greek word for fear is "phobos," which means fear, terror, or alarm.[14] Fear is false evidence appearing real. The enemy wants to keep the people of God in fear. He hates it when we find out who we are in Christ because we will become a big threat to his kingdom. He wants us

13. "fear" Merriam-Webster 2019, https://www.Merriam-Webster.com accessed 09-23-2019
14. Greek word for fear "phobos" https://www.biblehub.com accessed 09-23-2019

to be afraid to tell people about the Good News of Jesus so he can take as many people as he can to hell with him. But I beg to differ. Every time we go out of the house to the grocery store, restaurants and yes, even Walmart, God will give us a chance to advance His Kingdom. We have turned down many platforms because it wasn't behind a pulpit with a microphone. But Walmart, other grocery stores, and sporting events can be used as platforms to tell someone about the goodness of Jesus.

All you have to do is tell the people and lay the seed. He will send someone else to water the seed. Then He will give the increase. It is as simple as that. Also, there are many opportunities to pray for the same people in all those platforms. It seems like every time I go out on an errand, God gives me an opportunity to minister to someone or pray from them. I have had some refusals for prayer, but I haven't let it stop me. I continued to ask people if I can pray for them and most of them said, "Yes." This shows God's love for that person because you don't know what they were praying before they left home for the Lord to show them that He is real. Many people already don't feel like no one loves them, but when you obey the voice of God and pray for them, you give Satan a black eye. It will give them hope to make it through whatever they are going through at the time. So, don't let fear stop you from reaching out to the lost people in this world. God didn't just mean for us to only minister to the church people, but He meant for us to minister to the lost world. You don't have to worry about a title in front of your name or behind your name. Just do what God is calling you to do and that is to spread the Good News of Jesus to a lost and dying world.

DECLARATIONS (AMP)

For the Spirit of God does not make us timid, but gives us power, love, and self-discipline. (2 Timothy 1:7)

Be strong and courageous. (Deuteronomy 31:6)

Do not be afraid or terrified because of them for the Lord your God goes with you. (Deuteronomy 31:6)

He will never leave you nor forsake you. (Deuteronomy 31:6)

Even though I walk through the darkest valley, I will fear no evil. (Psalm 23:4)

Lord, for you are with me; your rod and your staff, they comfort me. (Psalm 23:4)

Who of you by worrying can add a single hour to your life? (Luke 12:25)

The Lord is my light and my salvation-- whom shall I fear? (Psalm 27:1)

The Lord is the stronghold of my life-- of who shall I be afraid? (Psalm 27:1)

The fear of the Lord is the beginning of wisdom. (Psalm 111:10)

So do not fear, for I am with you; do not be dismayed, for I am your God. (Isaiah 41:10)

Do not be afraid of those who kill the body but cannot kill the soul. (Matthew 10:28)

PRAYER

Father God, in the name of Jesus, I come before You today, asking that You touch my mind right now. Lord, help me to find confidence in You so I will not succumb to the spirit of fear in my life. I rebuke the stronghold of fear off my life right now. I command that all the little demons that are attached to this spirit be sent back to the abyss and be broken off my life. Satan, the blood of Jesus is against you and I cast out all your tormenting spirits to go back to the abyss in Jesus' name. Lord, release Your ministering angels to come and stand at my bedside when I am sleeping every night. I command my sleep to be sweet and I will rest soundly every night from this day forward in Jesus' name. I decree a good night's sleep on everyone who prays this prayer in Jesus' name. I command supernatural peace to surround them like a shield from this day forward in Jesus' name.

I command every tormenting spirit to go back to the abyss and be fettered with chains. Lord, thank You for the hedge of protection that You have erected around me and my family, home, and marriage in Jesus' name. Lord, You said in Your word that You would give us the peace that passeth all understanding and that You will guard my heart and mind in Jesus' name. Lord, thank You for loving me just that much to care about my rest. I speak peace to my mind and soul right now in Jesus' name. Amen.

CHAPTER SIX

Generational Curses

Merriam-Webster defines generational curses as a basis of defilement that has been passed down from one generation to the next.[15] In the Greek, curses means "katara," which means cursing, a curse, meton, or a doomed one.[16] Many curses and iniquities have come through family bloodlines.

15. "Generational curses" Merriam-Webster 2019, https://www.Merriam-Webster.com accessed 09-23-2019
16. Greek word for curses "katara" https://www.biblehub.com accessed 09-23-2019

Many generational curses haven't been dealt with, so they have been passed down to the third and fourth generations, as stated in Scripture. The enemy works to stay hidden through deception. He'll say that a Christian cannot have a demon, or that we have nothing that needs to be cast out. But that is a lie! Many Christians are demonically oppressed by many things that can be traced back to their great grandparents or that have trickled down through their bloodlines.

Many things have been swept under the rug instead of dealing with the matter or casting out the issue. That is why cancer seems to be running rampant in certain families because of undealt issues. Just because we ignore or don't acknowledge something, doesn't mean that it is not there. Nor does it mean that it won't show up later down the generational lineage. We must bind, cancel, and veto all generational curses to break them off the bloodline. It stops with you, and it will not go any further through the bloodline. It will not be transferred to your children or your children's children. It must be stopped, and you are the one who is going to stop it.

DECLARATIONS (KJV)

Lord, we repent for bowing down, worshipping, or serving other gods above You. (Exodus 20:5)

Thank You, Jesus, for redeeming us from the curse of the Law. (Galatians 3:13)

If the Son, therefore, shall make you free, ye shall be free indeed. (John 8:36)

I will bless them that bless thee, and curse him that curseth thee. (Genesis 12:3)

And in thee, all the families of the earth shall be blessed. (Genesis 12:3)

My people are destroyed for the lack of knowledge because thou has rejected knowledge. (Hosea 4:6)

And ye shall know the truth, and the truth shall make you free. (John 8:32)

Therefore, I say unto you, what things soever ye desire, when ye pray, believe that ye receive (them), and ye shall have (them). (Mark 11:24)

PRAYER

Father God, in the name of Jesus, I come before You today to ask that every generational curse back to Adam and Eve be broken off my life right now. Lord, we rebuke the stronghold of cancer off my bloodline from my mother's and my father's side of the family right now in Jesus' name. I will not die from cancer or any of its complications in Jesus' name. Lord, we break and bind every stronghold of inflammation, infirmities, and infections in our bodies and send them back to the abyss right now in Jesus' name. Lord, You said in Your Word that by Your stripes, we are healed in Jesus' name. I speak healing over my body right now in Jesus' name. I cancel and veto every word curse that has been spoken over me by myself, doctors, and other family members right now in Jesus' name. I receive the healing virtue of Jesus to saturate me from the top of my head to the soles of my feet. I bind high blood pressure, diabetes, lupus, and other sicknesses and diseases to go back to the one that sent it. I loose the blood of Jesus to cover me like a shield to keep the plots, plans, and ploys of the enemy at bay in my life. I render his power null and void. I loose the supernatural power of God to chain up the enemy from attacking my body and my bloodline right now in Jesus' name. Lord, I pray Psalm 91 as protection over everything that I own, my family, my bloodline, and everyone in my circle right now in Jesus' name. Amen.

CHAPTER SEVEN

Carnality

Carnality in the Merriam-Webster dictionary means to have a worldly mind, giving into pleasures and appetites of the world.[17] The Greek meaning of carnality is "sarkikos," which means pertaining to the flesh, fleshly, or earthly.[18]18 Revelation 3:16 (NIV) states, "So, because you are lukewarm--neither hot nor cold--I am about to spit you out of my mouth."

---

17. "carnality" Merriam-Webster 2019, https://www.Merriam-Webster.com accessed 09-23-2019
18. Greek word for carnality "sarkikos" https://www.biblehub.com accessed 09-23-2019

Lukewarm Christians care more about the matters of the world instead of taking care of God's business. Many of these Christians are still cursing and twisting Scriptures to justify their behavior. A true man or woman of God has no business cussing. If this is happening, they have not truly been born again. The grace of God is here to help us do what we can't do on our own. The world should be able to look at the people of God and see a difference in their lifestyle in us. Many Christians are trying to blend in with the world when God has mandated that we are to be set apart from it. We are living in the world, but there must be a difference between the clean and unclean in our lives. We should be striving every day to become more like Jesus in our walk on this earth.

All compromising spirits must die in a believer's life. We shouldn't be going along with anything that doesn't represent Christ in our lives, churches, and marriages. God is tired of some of the church leaders living worse than heathens. You would expect the world to be living sinfully, but some behind the pulpit who are supposed to be leading people to Christ are doing the opposite of what God intended. They must repent or face the consequences of the wrath of God in this dispensation. The judgment of God will begin in the house of God and it is already set in motion.

Declarations (NIV)

Lord, we repent for operating in the lusts of the flesh, and the lusts of the eyes, and the boastful pride of life, because it is not from the Father, but from the world. (1 John 2:16)

And be not conformed to this world, but be transformed by the renewing of your mind, so you may prove what the will of God is. (Romans 12:2)

For to set the mind governed by the flesh is death, but the mind governed by the Spirit is life and peace. (Romans 8:6)

The one who sows to please his flesh, from the flesh will reap destruction; but the one who sows to please the Spirit, from the Spirit will reap eternal life. (Galatians 6:8)

For if you live according to the flesh, you will die; but if by the Spirit you put to death the deeds of the body, you will live. (Romans 8:13)

For the wages of sin is death, but the gift of God is eternal life in Christ Jesus, our Lord. (Romans 6:23)

Because the carnal mind is enmity against God: for it is not subject to the law of God, neither indeed can be. (Romans 8:7,13)

For the kingdom of God is not meat and drink, but righteousness, and peace, and joy in the Holy Ghost. (Romans 14:17)

PRAYERS

Father God, in the name of Jesus, I come before You today to ask that You forgive me for any sins I may have committed knowingly and unknowingly, in thought and deed, in omission and commission right now. Lord, forgive me for not being obedient when You told me by your Spirit not to do a thing, but I did it anyway. Lord, help me to crucify my flesh so I will not continue to sin against You in Jesus' name. Lord, I desire to live a righteous and holy lifestyle from this day forward. Lord, remove the people who are bad influences and the ones who don't mean me any good out of my life. Lord, I give You permission to come into my heart and clean up my life from this day forward in Jesus' name. Lord, create in me a clean heart and renew a right spirit in me. I bind and cast out the spirit of carnality off my life and all its cohorts have to go back to the abyss right now in Jesus' name. Lord, I want to be serious about my relationship with You in Jesus' name. Lord, go deep down in my heart and soul. Remove everything that is not like you, Jesus. I no longer want to live as the old man, but I want to become a new creature in Christ Jesus. Lord, I thank You for deliverance and healing in Jesus' name. Amen.

CHAPTER EIGHT

Confusion

Confusion is an act of confusing or being baffled.[19] In Greek, the word for confusion is "akatastasia," which means disturbance, upheaval, and instability.[20] A confused person is unsure of what they should do next. The enemy wants to keep the people of God confused and unstable in their minds so they will react wrongly in certain situations. The spirit of confusion is not from

19. "confusion" Merriam-Webster 2019, https://www.Merriam-Webster.com accessed 09-24-2-19
20. Greek word for confusion "akatastasia" https://www.biblehub.com accessed 09-24-2019

God but is sent by the enemy to alter the average Christian from moving forward in godly matters. The enemy uses your diseased imagination to get you off the course that God has planned for your life. To keep our minds clear, we need to keep the helmet of salvation on our heads because it will repel the attacks of the enemy with foolishness. The enemy is the father of lies and nothing that he says or will ever say to you will be the truth. He has a way of stretching the truth in any given situation that you are facing. The enemy doesn't ever have anything positive to say to you or about you because he is trying his hardest to get you to walk away from God. But we must stay with God and ask Him to help us with the confusion that is plaguing our lives.

We cancel and veto the spirit of Dementia and Alzheimers that is sent by the enemy to make people forget who they are. These spirits start eating away at brain cells to the point that people cannot even remember what they did 30 minutes ago. It is sad to see these diseases take a person's memories of their families and anyone else that is close to them. These diseases have caused many people to commit suicide because they couldn't deal with being dependent on anyone else. We must pray the Scriptures, decree and declare what the Word says about this. We must continue to renew our minds with the Word of God to keep it strong and healthy. I believe that God is a mind regulator and He can heal you from both diseases that the medical field said was incurable. God can do anything but fail.

DECLARATIONS

For God is not the author of confusion, but of peace. (1 Corinthians 14:33 ESV)

Be alert and sober minded. (1 Peter 5:8 NIV)

Your enemy, the devil, prowls around like a roaring lion looking for someone to devour. (1 Peter 5:8 NIV)

Satan will not outwit us. (2 Corinthians 2:11 NIV)

For we are not unaware of his schemes. (2 Corinthians 2:11 NIV)

Submit yourselves, then, to God. Resist the devil, and he will flee from you. (James 4:7 NIV)

Satan is a liar and the father of liars. (John 8:44 NIV)

Trust in the Lord with all your heart and do not lean to your own understanding. (Proverbs 3:5 NIV)

I am of the Lord, the God of all mankind. Is anything too hard for me? (Jeremiah 32:27 NIV)

Do not fear, for I am with you, do not be dismayed, for I am your God. (Isaiah 41:10 NIV)

PRAYER

Father God, in the name of Jesus, I am crying out to you today to come and heal the broken places in my mind. Lord, You said in Psalm 107:20, "He sent his word and healed them. And delivered them from all of their destruction."

Lord, You also said in Jeremiah 33:6 that "Behold I will bring it health and healing; I will heal them and reveal to them the abundance of peace and truth." Lord, we speak peace to a confused mind right now in Jesus. Lord, let them find rest for their weary souls right now in Jesus' name. Lord, send your supernatural power to my brain and do a supernatural surgery on the part that controls my thoughts and memories. So that I will be able to remember everything that is important to me and you as well in Jesus' name. Lord, I speak healing to the cortex of my brain, and I command it to come into alignment with the Word of God. I cancel and veto every generational curse that has to do with memory loss and confusion right now in Jesus' name. I plead the blood of Jesus over my mind and I will have the mind of Christ with a photographic memory in Jesus' name. I will be able to remember important dates, birthdays, anniversaries, and all things that are important to me. I release my guardian angels to surround my mind with a shield of protection from Alzheimers, Dementia, and any other mind-altering diseases or illnesses in Jesus' name. Lord, I thank You for renewing my mind in Jesus' name. Amen.

CHAPTER NINE

Self-Sabotage

Self-Sabotage is an act or process tending to hamper or hurt.[21] In Greek, the word for sabotage is "sampotaz," which means deliberately destroy it.[22]22 In "40 day Soul Fast," Rebecca King stated that "It is easy in the rat race with life to become hard on ourselves. Many times, we have tried new things and they didn't work out for us, so we started feeling some type of way about ourselves. You have felt at times that you were

21. "self-sabotage" Merriam-Webster 2019, https://www.Merriam-Webster.com accessed 09-24-2019
22. Greek word for self-sabotage "sampotaz" https://www.biblehib.com accessed 09-24-2019

a failure and you couldn't seem to do anything right. But this is a trick of the enemy having you to talk down to yourself and put word curses on yourself. Just because what we tried didn't work the first two times doesn't mean that it won't be successful the 3rd time. The enemy wants us to fear the things that God wants us to do in the future, so he starts on us early by working on our self-esteem to get us off balance. But with God in our lives, He will give us the confidence we need to keep going and not give up.

Rebecca L. King also states in her book that, "God is not hard on us; therefore, we should not be hard on ourselves either. If anything, God wants to take our heaviness and deliver us from the evil of self- sabotage by being hard on ourselves."[23] We have to be willing to walk out in faith and fully trust God because He will not let you fail or give up on yourself. God loves us regardless of any past failures or mishaps that we have faced in our lives. God wants to make all things new in our lives. Just give your insecurities to Jesus and let Him help you work through them. You will be so glad that you released your worries and cares to

23   "40-day Soul Fast by Rebecca L. King 2015

Him. And you can do a lot of things and succeed at them. God has given us gifts and talents, so you don't have to feel inadequate about anything. Self-sabotage will no longer be an issue when you give God full control of your life. I bind and cast out all self-sabotaging spirits right now in Jesus' name. You will be all that God is calling you to be in Jesus' name. Amen.

DECLARATIONS (NIV)

I am the Lord, the God of all mankind. Is anything too hard for me? (Jeremiah 32:27)

But Jesus looked at them and said, "With man this is impossible, but with God all things are possible. (Matthew 19:26)

Is anything too difficult for the Lord? (Genesis 18:14)

Call to Me and I will answer and show you great and unsearchable things you do not know. (Jeremiah 33:3)

Take my yoke upon you and learn of Me, for I am gentle and humble in heart and you will find rest for your souls. (Matthew 11:29)

For my yoke is easy and my burden is light. (Matthew 11:29)

For our light affliction, which is but for a moment, worketh for us a far more exceeding and eternal weight of glory. (2 Corinthians 4:17)

Cast all your anxiety on Him because He cares for you. (1 Peter 5:7)

Who of you worrying can add a single hour to his life? (Matthew 6:27)

Be anxious for nothing, but everything by prayer and petition, with thanksgiving, present your requests to God. (Philippians 4:6)

PRAYER

Father, I come before You today to ask that You help remove the self-sabotaging spirit from my life right now in Jesus' name. Lord, I release it and lay it at your feet so that I can move on in You. Lord, I know now that there is a purpose and a calling on my life that You had planned for me when I was in my mother's womb. Lord, help me to give You all my worries and cares of the world so that I can move forward in my God-given destiny. Lord, I cancel and veto every generational curse from my father's and my mothers' side of the family that want me to feel stagnant in my life. I loose the freedom to move from one task to the other with the help of God.

Lord, I give You permission to come into my heart and mind and change the way that I think about myself. I cast down every word curse that has been spoken over my life by myself and family members. I render them null and void right now in Jesus' name. Self-sabotaging spirit, I am giving you notice that you will no longer control my life or hold me back from all that God has for me in Jesus' name. Lord, I thank You for breakthrough, healing, and deliverance in my emotions right now in Jesus' name. Lord, thank You for freedom, peace, joy, and Your unconditional love right now in Jesus name. Amen.

CHAPTER TEN

Anger

Anger, according to Merriam-Webster, is a strong feeling of displeasure and usually antagonism (opposition of a conflicting force, tendency, or principle).[24] In Greek, the word anger means "orge," which is anger, wrath, passion, punishment, or vengeance.[25] Ephesians 4:31-32 (AMP) says, "Let all bitterness and indignation and wrath (passion, rage, bad temper) and resentment(anger, animosity) and quarreling (brawling, clamor, contention) and slander (evil speaking, abusive or blasphemous language) be <u>banished from </u>you with all malice (spite, ill will).

24. "anger" Merriam-Webster 2019, https://www.Merriam-Webster.com accessed 09-24-2019

25. Greek word for anger "orge" https://www.biblehub.com accessed 09-24-2019

And become useful and helpful and kind to one another, tenderhearted (compassionate, understanding, loving heart) forgiving one another (readily and freely) as God in Christ forgave you."

Has the spirit of anger prevented you from moving forward in life? Learn to start forgiving others for offending or hurting you in the past and present. Have you allowed the spirit of anger to affect you and all your relationships? A study published in the Journal Behavioral Science & Law states that "9% of American adults or about 22 million people have a history of impulsive angry behavior and have access to at least one gun. About 1.5% of people or about 3.7 million people with impulsive anger issues carry guns around with them when they are outside of their homes." The adults in this study admit that they lose their temper to the point of having uncontrollable "tantrums" which sometimes includes breaking or smashing things and getting into physical fights.[26] In chapter four of "It Cost Me Everything," by Prophetess Kimberly Moses, several co-authors, and myself, talked

26. Journal behavioral Science & Law Statistics on anger accessed 09-24-2019

about all the repercussions of not dealing with anger. Anger is a spiritual problem that must be dealt with, so we can live peaceful lives with our spouses, families, friends, co-workers and whoever that we may meet. Romans 12:18 (AMP) says, "If possible as far as it depends on you, live at peace with everyone." Are you ready to receive deliverance from always getting angry at everything and everybody to living a peaceful life here on this earth? Anger is a destiny stopping spirit that must be broken. Now we have seen some of the statistics that comes from not dealing with uncontrollable anger.[27]

DECLARATIONS (AMP)

A happy heart is good medicine and a joyful mind causes healing. (Proverbs 17:22)

---

27. "It Cost Me Everything "Anger" by Prophetess Kimberly Moses and Co-Authors March 2019 accessed 09-24-2019.

A broken spirit dries up the bones. (Proverbs 17:22)

Bearing graciously with one another, and willingly forgiving each other. (Colossians 3:13)

Watch over your heart with all diligence, for from it flows the springs of life. (Proverbs 4:23)

Put from you a deceitful (lying, misleading mouth), And put devious lips from you. (Proverbs 4:24)

Beloved, never avenge yourselves, but leave the way open for God's wrath (and judicial righteousness); for it is written (in scripture), Vengeance is mine, I will repay, says the Lord. (Romans 12:19)

Living as becomes you with complete lowliness of mind (humility) and meekness (unselfishness), gentleness, mildness) with patience bearing with one another. (Ephesians 4:2 AMPC)

Be eager and strive earnestly to guard and keep the harmony and oneness of (and produced by) the Spirit in binding power of peace. (Ephesians 4:3 AMPC)

And that the peace of God (that peace which reassures the heart, that peace) which transcends all understanding (that peace which) stand guard over your hearts and minds in Christ Jesus (is yours). (Philippians 4:7)

And forgive us our debts, as we forgive our debtors (letting go of both the wrong and the resentment). (Matthew 6:12)

PRAYER

Dear Heavenly Father, I come before You today, asking that You help me remove the spirit of anger that is trying to consume my life in Jesus' name. Lord, help me to be able to forgive everyone that has ever hurt or disappointed me in my childhood up until this present time. I repent for letting the devil use me to take the bait of the offense and not walking in forgiveness in Jesus' name. Lord, You said in Matthew 6:12 (AMP), "And forgive us our debts, as we forgive our debtors (letting go of both the wrong and the resentment)." Help me to release bitterness, resentment, retaliation, bad attitudes, unforgiveness, and frustrations so there won't be any sicknesses or diseases that may try to attach itself to my body in Jesus' name. Lord, You said in Psalms 91:10 (AMPC), "There shall no evil befall you, nor any plague or calamity come near your tent." Lord, I realize that forgiving the person of the offense will help me walk closer to You in Jesus' name. Lord, I veto and cancel all anger in my life and any consequences that come with it in Jesus' name. I speak life into me right now. I will live and not die and declare the works of the Lord in Christ Jesus. I will move forward in the things of God in Jesus' name. I will walk in freedom, joy, peace, and love in every area of my life from this day forward. I will rest in Your presence and lay all my trials and disappointments at Your feet for You to handle in Jesus' name. Amen.

CHAPTER ELEVEN

Addiction

Addiction is a compulsive, chronic, physiological or psychological need for a habit-forming substance, behavior, to indulge into something repeatedly.[28] In Greek, the word addiction is "prosecho," which means to hold to or turn to.[29] You can be addicted to many things such as drugs, sex, alcohol, or food. It is anything that you over-indulge in that causes the problem. Because too much of anything is not good for you unless it is

28. addiction" Merriam-Webster 2019, https://www.Merriam-Webster.com accessed 09-24-2019
29. Greek word for addiction "prosecho" https://www.biblehub.com accessed 09-24-2019

Jesus. We know that we can never have too much Jesus in our lives. The above listed addictions start out seemingly innocent. Then as we continue to indulge without restraints, it becomes a big problem in our lives. When any of these things start affecting how you live and function. Ultimately, it has become a habit that needs to be broken. The enemy wants to get you hooked on these things so that he will have a hold on you. If you are not careful, you could lose your families, jobs, homes, and your self-respect behind addictions. Addictions will take you to a dark place, and it has made many people feel like they are not needed in the world. Many have committed suicide with all types of drugs.

Sometimes I watch a show on TV where you are riding with the police as they respond to their calls. There are many instances where people have Overdose (OD) on some drugs. And the paramedics must give them a drug called Narcan to bring people back to life after they have gotten lethargic and stopped breathing. Drugs or anything that alters the state of mind are dangerous if not taking it properly. Alcohol is another dangerous drug that can cause a person to go from a social drinker to an alcoholic because they must drink every day to be able to function. Sex is dangerous, especially with all these sexually transmitted diseases that are out here. Two minutes of pleasure is not worth a lifetime of HIV or AIDS. These two are deadly diseases that are transferred from having unprotected sex. These diseases have destroyed many lives and families. But the God that we serve, Jesus can heal, deliver, and set us free all these addictions. But a person must come to Jesus and give their life completely over to Him. I have read testimonies where God has healed HIV and AIDS. That is a miracle. Also, I have heard where people have been a full-blown alcoholic and God delivered them. He took the taste from their mouths and they never drank another drop of alcohol. So, God is the answer to all addictions. When they find out that God really does love them, and they start loving themselves. Then they can move past these addictions to freedom in God.

DECLARATIONS (NIV)

No temptation has overtaken you, except what is common to mankind. (1 Corinthians 10:13)

And God is faithful; he will not let you be tempted beyond what you can bear. (1 Corinthians 10:13)

But when you are tempted. He will also provide a way out so that you can endure it. (1 Corinthians 10:13)

Therefore, my dear friends, flee from idolatry. (1 Corinthians 10:14)

For everything in the world--the lust of the flesh, the lust of the eyes, and the pride of life-- comes not from the Father but from the world. (1 John 2:16)

Do not be misled: Bad company corrupts good character. (1 Corinthians 15:33)

Submit yourselves, then, to God. Resist the devil, and he will flee from you. (James 4:7)

And call on me in the day of trouble, I will deliver you, and you will honor me. (Psalm 50:15)

God himself will restore you and make you strong, firm, and steadfast. (1 Peter 5:10)

I have the right to do anything--but I will not be mastered by anything. (1 Corinthians 6:12)

PRAYER

Father God, in the name of Jesus, I come before You today to lift up everyone that has some addiction, whether it be to sex, food, drugs, and alcohol. Lord, we pray that You break all these destiny stopping spirits right now in Jesus' name. I bind the stronghold of addiction off the lives of Your people in Jesus' name. I loose freedom, peace, love over every one of them that are truly crying out to You Lord for deliverance. Father,

I ask that You send Your ministering angels to minister to them right now in Jesus' name. Lord, let them feel Your love like never before in their lives right now in Jesus' name. Lord, let them know that You are not mad at them. You want them to be healed, delivered, and set free from the darkness that is trying to consume them in Jesus' name. Lord, You said in Your Word that the prayers of the righteous availeth much and produce wonderful results. So, we are asking that You make all things new in their lives. Lord, go deep down in their hearts and heal every broken and wounded place so they can be truly free. Lord, touch and soften their hardened hearts. Remove the heart of stone and give them a heart of flesh right now in Jesus' name. Lord, we ask that You save and fill each one of them with Your Holy Ghost and power in Jesus' name. Lord, help them to start loving themselves the way that You love them. Lord, we thank You for intervening in everyone's life today who wants to change for the better in Christ Jesus. Lord, we love you and ask this right now in Jesus' name. Amen.

CHAPTER TWELVE

Depression

Depression is defined as an act of depressing, or a state of being sad or depressed.[30] The Greek word for depression is "tapeinosis," which is a low state, humiliation, or be made low.[31] Statistics estimates that 20% of adults will experience at least one bout of serious clinical depression in their lifetime.[32]

---

30. "depression" Merriam-Webster 2019, https://www.Merriam-Webster.com accessed 09-24-2019
31. Greek word for depression "tapeinosis" hhtps://www.biblehub.com accessed 09-24-2019
32. www.ask-angels.com, statistics for depression https://www.ask-angels.com accessed 09-25-2019

Many are facing a lifelong struggle with depression. Depression is more than just a miserable day here and there. It is more than disappointments because you didn't get the job, the guy, the girl, or a dream house. Someone suffering from depression faces a daily battle against hopelessness. Depression is when you seem to lose all sense of joy derived from things you used to enjoy doing. Now they have become meaningless to you. God wants to deliver you from this form of oppression before it destroys your life and the lives of others know.[33] The enemy (Satan) wants to keep us in darkness and feeling like we have nothing to live for. The enemy came to steal, kill, and destroy you. But you must release all that pent-up frustration and lay it at Jesus' feet.

God loves and wants the best for us. Jesus came to give us life and life more abundantly, so that means He wants us to have a healthy emotional and mental well-being. I have learned to stop worrying about things that I have no control

---

33. "Walking In Total Freedom After Healing From Deep Inner Wounds" by LaRose Angela Richardson accessed 09-25-2019.

over. Also, I learned to truly trust God to take care of my family and me. When this truth became a reality for me, it truly gave me a peace of mind about my whole life. My life is in God's hands. He wants you to turn over your life to Him so that He can work things out for your good as well. The only way to true peace of mind is through a relationship with Jesus because He is the Prince of Peace. The world doesn't have lasting peace. Only in Jesus Christ can you find true lasting peace. You will still have trials and tribulations, but during the storm, you will be in perfect peace. Give Him your troubles, problems, and issues today and watch Him work them out for you.

DECLARATIONS (NIV)

The Lord Himself goes before you and will be with you. (Deuteronomy 31:8)

He will never leave or forsake you. (Deuteronomy 31:8)

Do not be afraid; do not be discouraged. (Deuteronomy 31:8)

The righteous cry out, and the Lord hears them; he delivers them from all their troubles. (Psalm 34:17)

I waited patiently for the Lord; he turned to me and heard my cry. (Psalm 40:1)

He lifted me out of the slimy pit, out of the mud and mire; he set my feet on a rock and gave me a firm place to stand. (Psalm 40:2)

He put a new song in my mouth, a hymn of praise to our God. (Psalm 40:3)

Many will see and fear the Lord and put their trust in him. (Psalm 40:3)

But you, Lord, are a shield around me, my glory, the One who lifts my head high. (Psalm 3:3)

Put your hope in God, for I will yet praise him, my Savior and my God. (Psalm 42:11)

PRAYER

Father God, in the name of Jesus, I come before You today, asking that You would remove this spirit of depression from my life. Lord, I cast my cares on you because you care for me. Lord, I am tired of not getting enough of the proper rest at night and worrying about things that I have no control over. Lord, help me to trust Your will in all the aspects of my life in Jesus' name. I bind the stronghold of depression and all the symptoms that come with it. I command it to go back to the abyss and get out of my life. I loose peace that passeth all understanding over my life from this day forward.

Lord, help me to remember how much you love and care for my family and me. I know now that You have my best interest at heart. I bind the spirit of not enough because I know with You Jesus, I am more than enough in You. I bind the spirit of suicide and all its symptoms out of my life right now in Jesus' name. I speak life and life more abundantly over my life and mind. I will live and not die and declare the works of the Lord. I am more than a conqueror if I keep my hand in Your hand God. Lord, I give You permission to come into my heart and change it for the better in Jesus' name. Lord, create in me a clean heart and renew a right spirit in me in Jesus' name. I will have the mind of Christ. Lord, I plead the blood of Jesus over my mind and through life in Jesus' name. Lord, thank You for giving me a new lease on life and realizing that I have everything to live for in Jesus' name. Amen.

CHAPTER THIRTEEN

Faith

Faith is the allegiance to duty or a person, loyalty, a belief and trust in loyalty to God.[34] The Greek word for faith is "pistis," which means faith, faithfulness, trust, confidence, or belief. [35] Hebrews 11:1-5 (NIV) states, "Now faith is confidence in what we hope for and assurance about what we do not see." [2]. "This is what the ancients (saints before us) were commended for." [3]. "By faith we understand that the universe was formed

34. "faith" Merriam-Webster 2019 https://www.Merriam-Webster. com accessed 09-25-2019
35. Greek word for faith "pistis" https://www.biblehub.com accessed 09-25-2019

at God's command, so that what is seen was not made out of what was visible." [4.] "By faith Abel brought a better offering than Cain did. By faith he was commended as righteous when God spoke well of his offerings. and by faith Abel still speaks, even though he is dead." [5.] "By faith Enoch was taken from this life, so that he did not experience death: "He could not be found, because God had taken him away. "For before he was taken, he was commended as one who pleased God."

Faith is a gift from God given to believers. Faith for the believer is God's divine persuasion and therefore, distinct from human belief. Faith is only (exclusively) given to the redeemed. It is not a virtue that can be worked up by human effort. We need faith to be able to operate in the Kingdom of God. Because we first must believe that Jesus is the Son of God before we can receive sanctification. We need faith to be able to activate the grace of God. We have to believe that grace is more than unmerited favor, but it is the ability to do what we can't do on our own. All of this is activated through our faith in God. When God works miracles in our lives, our faith increases to a whole new level. That is why we need to tell our testimonies every chance we are given because it helps others believe God for their lives. Revelation 12:11 (NIV) states, "They triumphed over him by the blood of the Lamb and by the word of their testimony; they did not love their lives so much as to shrink from death." This whole Christian walk is a faith walk. We need faith for everything that concerns the Kingdom and our lives.

DECLARATIONS (NIV)

And without faith it is impossible to please God. (Hebrews 11:6)

Because anyone who comes to Him must believe that He exists and that He rewards those who earnestly seek Him. (Hebrews 11:6)

God is our refuge and strength, and ever-present help in trouble. (Psalm 46:1)

Now may the Lord of peace Himself give you peace at all times and in every way. (2 Thessalonians 3:16)

The Lord be with all of you. (2 Thessalonians 3:16)

But you, Lord, do not be far from me. (Psalm 22:19)

You are my strength, come quickly to help me. (Psalm 22:19)

I have told you these things, so that in me you may have peace. (John 16:33)

In this world you will have trouble. But take heart! I have overcome the world. (John 16:33)

The name of the Lord is a fortified tower, the righteous run to it and are safe. (Proverbs 18:10)

PRAYERS

Father God, in the name of Jesus, I come to You today to lay all my cares on You because You care for me. Lord, help me increase my faith in You to believe for the impossible situations in my life right now in Jesus' name. Lord, You said in Your Word that without faith that it was impossible to please You. So, since I desire to please You, help my unbelief. Lord, You said in Mark 11:23 (NIV) "Truly I tell you, if anyone says to this mountain, Go, throw yourself into the sea; and does not doubt in their heart but believes that what they say will happen. it will be done for them." So, according to Your Word, I come into agreement with it. I know that You are going to do it once I speak it in Jesus' name.

Lord, You also said in Matthew 17:20 (NIV), "Truly I tell you, if you have faith as small as a mustard seed, you can say to this mountain, Move from here to there; and it will move. Nothing will be impossible for you." Lord, now I can have the faith for you to save all my family members who don't know You as their Savior right now in Jesus' name. Lord, I can believe You for healing in my body and mind, according to Your Word. Lord, I have faith to believe that all my trials have an expiration date because You didn't intend for them to be permanent in my life or my families' lives. Lord, I know that faith is like a muscle. The more I use it, the stronger it will become. So, I continue to believe You for all my needs in Jesus' name. Amen.

CHAPTER FOURTEEN

Lying

Lying is defined by a marked or containing untrue statement, or false.[36] In the Greek, lying is "pseudomai." Lying means to deceive, lie, speak falsely, or to falsify.[37] Lying is a terrible thing to do. Some people get up every day with the intention of deceiving people out of their property, money, etc. The spirit of lying should be a thing of the past once a person comes to Christ. We should be striving daily to get rid of

36. "lying" Merriam-Webster 2019 https://www.Merriam-Webster accessed 09-25-2019
37. Greek word for lying "pseudomai" https://www.biblehub.com accessed 09-25-2019

that spirit. Some women lie about being a young-er age. We need to embrace our age because it is a blessing to live to see 60 years old. I know people who didn't live to see even that age. So, we must be careful that we always tell the truth and walk in integrity at all times. Lying on taxes is another problem. We will lie and say we have children when we know that we don't just to get more money from the government. Usually, the money doesn't last long because it was gotten by ill gain. We must repent daily because we may have misquoted something. If we make a mistake about something, no matter what it is, we need to correct it.

You may be getting more money, but you are grieving the Holy Spirit in the process. Also, if we say we are going to do something and a situ-ation arises where we can't, we should make an effort to let someone know that we can't do it for whatever reason instead of letting it go unex-plained. When someone is selling something and you don't want it, then don't say, "Maybe I will get one next time," knowing you aren't planning on getting the item. Stop wasting people's time and tell them the truth the first time that they ask you about it.

Matthew 12:36 (NIV) says, "But I tell you that everyone will have to give account on the day of judgment for every empty word they have spoken." It is so much easier to tell the truth. A person that has a lying spirit must have a good memory because they usually forget what they have said previously and get caught in lies. Some people can look you dead in the eyes and lie. God will give you the discernment to know when they are lying. God wants people delivered from this spirit because He has to be able to trust them before He allows them to do things for the Kingdom of God. Just be trustworthy. Lord, we repent for every time that we didn't tell the truth, for whatever reason. Lord, help us to be truthful so we can be glory carriers and live a life of integrity in all our dealings in this world. If we have lied in the past about anything, give us the wisdom to make it right from this day forth.

DECLARATIONS (NIV)

Do not steal. Do not lie. Do not deceive one another. (Leviticus 19:11)

The Lord detests lying lips, but he delights in people are trustworthy. (Proverbs 12:22)

The righteous hate what is false, but the wicked make themselves a stench and bring shame on themselves. (Proverbs 13:5)

An honest witness does not deceive, but a false witness pours out lies. (Proverbs 14:5)

Eloquent lips are unsuited to a godless fool-- how much worse lying lips to a ruler! (Proverbs 17:7)

They will do no wrong; they will tell no lies. A deceitful tongue will not be found in their mouths. (Zephaniah 3:13)

Then Peter said, "Ananias, how is that Satan has so filled your heart that you lied to the Holy Spirit and have kept for yourself some of the money you received for the land? (Acts 5:3)

Do not let unwholesome talk come out of your mouths, but only what is helpful for building others up according to their needs, that it may benefit those who listen. (Ephesians 4:29)

Do not lie to each other, since you have taken off your old self with its practices. (Colossians 3:9)

No one who practices deceit will dwell in my house; no one who speaks falsely will stand in my presence. (Psalm 101:7)

PRAYER

Father God, in the matchless name of Jesus, I come before You today to ask for forgiveness for lying about things when I should be telling the truth. Lord, You said in Your Word that a liar would not tarry in your sight. Lord, I need Your grace to help me start telling the truth regardless of the outcome. Lord, I don't want anything to block or hinder my walk with You. I want to be a trustworthy person and let my word stand for truth and not falsehood. Lord, I bind and cast out every generational curse of lying that goes all the way back to my mother's and father's side of the family. This lying spirit is rendered null and void. It will not destroy another generation because it stops with me. I plead the blood of Jesus over my mind, mouth, and tongue. Lord, I ask you to anoint my tongue, so the only thing that will be uttered from it will be the truth from now on. Lord, You said in Psalm 52:2 (Berean Study Bible), "Your tongue devises destruction like a sharpened razor, O worker of deceit."

Lord, I activate with my faith and the fruit of the Spirit where self-control is an important part of it. Lord, help me bridle my tongue and keep it off people. Psalm 39:1 (NIV) states, "I will watch my ways and keep my tongue from sin; I will put a muzzle on my mouth while in the presence of the wicked." Lord, if an evil thought should arise in my mind, help me to suppress it. Help me to keep silent and meditate on Your Word instead of reacting when an evil thought arises in my mind.

Lord, enlighten my mind by your Holy Spirit. Fill my heart with Your grace, so I will know when to speak and when to be quiet. Lord, let self-control saturate me from the top of my head to the soles of my feet in Jesus' name. Lord, may everything I do from this day forth, glorify Your name in Jesus' name. Amen.

CHAPTER FIFTEEN

Lust

Lust is defined as usually intense, or unbridled sexual desire, and intense longing craving.[38] In the Greek, the word lust is "epithumia," which means desire, passionate longing, lust, or inordinate desire.[39] Lust is born of Satan and the flesh. Lust is something that a man or woman may do to another person of the opposite sex, or they could be lusting after material things as well. But in the new age era now, you have men lusting after

38. "lust" Merriam-Webster 2019 https://www.Merriam-Webster accessed 09-25-2019
39. Greek word for lust "epithumia" https://www.biblehub.com accessed 09-25-2019

men and women lusting after women. The enemy (Satan) wants to advance his agenda with a counterfeit love that opposes what God intended for this world. We can witness this by looking at the news and certain television shows. Some cartoons are meant to confuse the little preschool kids about their sexuality by trying to get them to lean toward a homosexual lifestyle. A young child doesn't know anything about the subject of sexuality. We, as parents and grandparents, must be attentive to what our children and grandchildren are watching on television and what they are doing on the internet.

The enemy wants everyone to think that he has the upper hand, but in reality, he doesn't. I like to give a wakeup call to all parents and grandparents that they need an effective prayer life. They need to be praying for the next generation because the enemy wants to start working on them young. So that means that we need to start early teaching them about God, who He is, how to pray and cover themselves with prayer. Purchase a book with all the Bible stories in it so we can teach and read it to them regularly. As they get older, let them read it to you. Because the Word of God states,

"Train up a child in the way that they should go and when they get old, they will not depart from the faith. They need to put the Word into them, so the Spirit of God can have something to bring back to their remembrance. No more putting the responsibility on the parents if they don't know God. If the grandparents do know the Lord, then it's their mandate to teach their grandchildren the truth about God.

There will come a time when we may have to stop watching certain shows because the enemy has subliminal messages in them. For instance, if you watch movies or television shows with sexual scenes, then the next thing you are thinking about is sex. So, the enemy believes that if he can show the young children that, then it is alright. He wants them to like the same sex in subliminal messages on television shows, so they will start having a curiosity (strong desire to learn or know something), and they will eventually act upon it. But the devil is a liar. He will not destroy another generation with his lies.

DECLARATIONS

But I tell you that anyone who looks at a woman lustfully has already committed adultery with her in his heart. (Matthew 5:28 NIV)

Flee the evil desires of youth and pursue righteousness, faith, love and peace, along with those who call on the Lord out of a pure heart. (2 Timothy 2:22 NIV)

For everything in the world-the lust of the flesh, the lust of the eyes, and the pride of life--comes not from the Father but from the world. (1 John 2:16 NIV)

Do not lust in your heart after beauty or let her captivate you with her eyes. (Proverbs 6:25 NIV)

So, I say, walk by the Spirit, and you will not gratify the desires of the flesh. (Galatians 5:16 NIV)

The mind governed by the flesh is death, but the mind governed by the Spirit is life and peace. (Romans 8:6 NIV)

But each person is tempted when they are dragged away by their own desire and enticed. (James 1:14 NIV)

Let no man say when he is tempted, "I am tempted by God; for God cannot be tempted by evil, and He Himself does not tempt anyone. (James 1:13)

But I discipline my body and make it my slave, so that, after I have preached to others, I myself will not be disqualified. (1 Corinthians 9:27 Berean Study Bible)

Now that those who belong to Christ Jesus have crucified the flesh with its passions and desires. (Galatians 5:24 NASB)

PRAYERS

Father God, in the name of Jesus, I come before You today to ask for You to help me bring my body under subjection to your Holy Spirit. Lord, I will be careful of what my children, grandchildren, and I are watching on television so no demonic seeds will be planted in our subconscious in Jesus' name. Lord, I pray that You would give me wisdom and understanding of the things that You need for me to be doing instead of watching something that is meant to destroy me and my walk with you. Lord, I call forth the Holy Ghost filled writers to write and produce television shows and cartoons that don't try to lead our children astray from the truth of Your word in Jesus' name.

Lord, You said in Your Word, "That the prayers of the righteous availeth much and produce wonderful results" in Jesus' name. So, I know that if I keep praying for the entertainment industry that You will send some of Your people to write and produce good and wholesome shows for our children to watch in Jesus' name. Lord, we thank

You for the movies that are already out that stand up for You and Your Word in Jesus' name. Lord, I thank You for caring about the show and the movies that Your children are watching in Jesus' name. Lord, thank You in advance of what is to come in Jesus' name. Amen.

CHAPTER SIXTEEN

Ungodly Soul Ties

Merriam-Webster defines the soul as the moral and emotional nature of human beings, sentiment, or a person's total self.[40] The Greek word for soul is "psyche," which means the vital breath of life, the human soul, the seat of affections and will.[41] Merriam-Webster defines ties as attach or

40. "ungodly soul ties" Merriam-Webster 2019 https://www. Merriam-Webster.com accessed 09-25-2019

41. Greek word for soul "psyche" https://www.biblehub.com accessed 09-25-2019

fasten, restrict or limit (someone) to a particular situation.[42] In the Greek, ties means "deo" which means to tie or bind, or fasten.[43] Terry Savelle Foy states that if you have been tormented by thoughts about a person, excessively wondering about them, checking on them, rehearsing times with them, then you have a soul tie if you answered yes to all these things. Soul ties are formed through close relationships, through vows, commitments and promises, and through physical intimacy. Not all soul ties are bad. God wants us to have healthy relationships that build us up, provide wisdom, give Godly counsel. God will strategically bring good relationships into our lives to form healthy soul ties. But Satan always brings counterfeits into our lives to form unhealthy soul ties. Here are a few ways unhealthy soul ties can be formed:

- Abusive Relationships (physically, sexually, emotionally, verbally)
- Adulterous affairs
- Sex before Marriage

42. "ties" Merriam-Webster 2019 https://www.Merriam-Webster.com accessed 09-25-2019
43. Greek word for ties "deo" https://www.biblehub.com accessed 09-25-2019

- Obsessive entanglements with a person (giving them more authority in your life than you give to God)
- Controlling Relationships

If you have any ungodly soul ties right now, no matter how painful it is, you need deliverance to get free from them so you can move forward in your life. There is no need to stay miserable inside our hearts when God wants us delivered and free from all ungodly soul ties. Don't go another day, month, or year struggling to obey the instructions of God. Remember, partial obedience is still disobedience, especially if He has told you to break all ties, communication with this person and you refuse to do so. Delayed obedience is still disobedience. Do what God is telling you to do because it's always for your benefit. God is not trying to hurt you. He is trying to help you. He sees what you don't see about a person or situation. You will never regret obeying God. Never. Your life isn't over because a relationship is over. God wants you to let go of the past and get on a pursuit of Him. God has big dreams for your life.[44]

44. article "Ungodly Soul Ties by Terri Savelle accessed 09-28-2019

DECLARATIONS

But he who unites himself with the Lord is one with him in spirit. (1 Corinthians 6:17 Berean Study Bible)

Wherefore come out from among and be ye separate, saith the Lord, and touch not the unclean thing; and I will receive you. (2 Corinthians 6:17)

For you are the temple of the living God. As God has said, I will dwell in them, and walk in them; and I will be their God, and they shall be my people. (2 Corinthians 6:16)

Be not unequally yoked with unbelievers; for what fellowship have righteousness and iniquity? (2 Corinthians 6:14 ASV)

Or what communion has light with darkness? (2 Corinthians 6:14 AKJV)

Flee from sexual immorality. All other sins a man commits are outside the body, but whoever sins sexually sins against his own body. (1 Corinthians 6:18 NIV)

For the word of God is quick, and powerful, and sharper than any two-edged sword, piercing even to the dividing asunder of soul and spirit, and of the joints and marrow. (Hebrews 4:12)

The Word of God is a discerner of the thoughts and intents of the heart. (Hebrews 4:12)

PRAYER

Father God, in the name of Jesus, I break every ungodly soul tie that I have with anyone in my past right now in Jesus' name. God, I thank You for sending your Son to die for me. He rose again with all power in the palm of His hand so that I can be free today. I cancel and veto every soul tie off my family all the way back to Adam and Eve and up to this present time in Jesus' name. I break any bondages that have been formed in my life due to any soul ties that I picked up through previous relationships in Jesus' name. I break and cast out any obsessive spirit that may have transferred to me by past partners in Jesus' name. Lord, I plead the blood of Jesus over me and any soul ties that are trying to destroy my life in Jesus' name. Lord, I make a circle around my family and me with your blood so that no demonic oppressive spirits can continue to attack us. Lord, I cover every unholy soul tie and I cast them out of my life from this day forward in Jesus' name. I plead the blood of Jesus over my body, soul, emotions, and will in Jesus' name. Lord, I welcome the Holy Spirit to come into my heart and take up residence from this day forward in Jesus' name. I decree that I will have a pure heart and I will have the mind of Christ in Jesus' name. Lord, thank You for setting me free in Jesus' name. Amen.

CHAPTER SEVENTEEN

Witchcraft

Witchcraft is the use of sorcery or magic, and communication with the devil.[45] The Greek word for witchcraft is "pharmakeia," which is the use of medicine, drugs, spells, sorcery, or enchantment.[46] This word can mean many things in this day and age. Today street drugs are running rampant through generations. Some are heroin, marijuana, and other drugs that are laced with methamphetamines that makes people do crazy

45. "witchcraft" Merriam-Webster 2019 https://www.Merriam-Webster.com accessed 09-28-2019
46. Greek word for witchcraft "pharmakeia" https://www.biblehub.com accessed 09-28-2019

and irrational things. Some people have started to abuse prescriptions like pain medicines such as Vicodin, Lorcet, Darvocet, Xanax, and Ativan. They will use anything that will alter their mental status and cause them to get a high. The only problem with any of these drugs is you never get the high again like you did when you first tried them. So that is one of the reasons many people have become so addicted because they have to keep taking more and more drugs, trying to chase after the first initial high that they experienced. That is why drugs are a form of witchcraft because of the destiny destroying power they have on the user.

The next kind of witchcraft is in people who have the gift of prophecy, but they are using their gift for the devil instead of God. You will always see the enemy come up with a counterfeit with everything that God is doing in the earth and witchcraft is one of them. Witches and warlocks are talking to demons about the things that people go to them to seek answers for their lives. But through prophetic ministry, the person who is giving the prophecy is getting all the information from the Holy Spirit as they tell an individual about what the Lord wants them to know concerning the plans that He has for their lives. The power of God is so much powerful and stronger than any familiar spirit that a witch or warlock could ever conjure up. The blood of Jesus is all powerful and it covers the life of a child of God. That is why prayer is so important and having an intimate relationship with Christ because the covering that surrounds you like a shield cannot be infiltrated if you keep the connection open between you and God. The Word of God states, "No weapon formed against us will prosper." It may form but God has a shield of protection around every believer. All we have to do is live a life that is pleasing to Him and our protection is guaranteed by His Word and blood.

DECLARATIONS

Do not turn to medium or necromancers; do not seek them out, and so make yourselves unclean by them: I am the Lord your God. (Leviticus 19:31)

You shall not permit a sorceress to live. (Exodus 22:18)

A man or a woman who is a medium or a necromancer shall surely be put to death. (Leviticus 20:27)

He will cover you with his feathers, and under his wings you will find refuge; his faithfulness will be your shield and rampart. (Psalm 91:4 NIV)

Dear children you belong to God. So, you have won the victory over these people, because the one who is in you is greater than the one who is in the world. (1 John 4:4)

We know that God's children do not make a practice of sinning, for God's Son holds them securely, and the evil one cannot touch them. (1 John 5:18 NLT)

But the Lord is faithful; he will strengthen you and guard you from the evil one. (2 Thessalonians 3:3 Berean Study Bible)

The Lord keeps you from all harm and watches over your life. (Psalm 121:7 NLT)

The Lord keeps watch over you as you come and go, both now and forever. (Psalm 121:8 NLT)

But whoever listens to me will live in safety. and be at ease, without fear of harm. (Proverbs 1:33 NIV)

"My son if you receive my words and treasure up my commandments with you. (Proverbs 2:1 NASB)

The fear of the Lord leads to life; one will sleep at night without danger. (Proverbs 19:23 HCSB)

PRAYER

Father God, in the name of Jesus, we come before You today to ask that You would keep me protected under your wings from any form of witchcraft right now in Jesus' name. I trust You to be able to keep me protected because of the love that You have for me. Psalm 91:9-10 (NIV) says, "The Lord is my refuge. I will make the Most

High my dwelling. No harm will overtake me. No disaster will come near my tent." Lord, I thank You for Your covering and protection that You have over me from this day forward. Lord, You said in Ecclesiastes 8:5 (NIV), "Whoever obeys His command will come to no harm, and the wise heart will know the proper time and procedure." Thanks for rescuing me and protecting those who trust in Your name. Lord, I pray Psalm 91 over my life and the lives of my loved ones. I know that we are covered under your blood, so no hurt, harm, or danger will come our way.

Lord, You also said in Isaiah 54:17, "that coming day no weapon turned against us will prosper and that You will silence every voice that has risen against me because this is the heritage of the saints in Christ Jesus." Lord, I thank You for being God in my life in Jesus' name. Lord, You said in Your word to suffer the witch to die. You also said that we could cut every silver cord on the ones that try to astral project into our rooms and houses during the night hours to torment us in Jesus' name. Amen.

CHAPTER EIGHTEEN

Unbelief/Doubt

Unbelief can be defined as skepticism in faith or disbelief.[47] In the Greek, unbelief is "apistia," which means unbelief and distrust.[48] Doubt is to call a question to the truth of, or to be uncertain.[49] In the Greek, the word doubt is "distazo" which means to waver, hesitate, or shifting between positions.[50]

47. "Unbelief/Doubt" Unbelief Merriam-Webster 2019 https://www.Merriam-Webster.com accessed 09-28-2019
48. Greek word for unbelief "apistia" https://www.biblehib.com accessed 09-28-2019'
49. "doubt" Merriam Webster 2019 https://www.Merriam-Webster.com accessed 09-28-2019
50. Greek word for doubt" distazo" https://www.biblehub.com ac-

Unbelief and doubt run hand in hand because if you doubt something, then the reality of the matter is that you don't really believe it to be true. That is why you are questioning the accuracy of a matter because of unbelief. In the Bible, Jesus couldn't do many miracles in His hometown because of unbelief. They were looking at His earthly identity instead of His heavenly one. If we could see things in the spiritual realm instead of always looking in the natural realm, then we can see the already manifested blessings. It will be a matter of time before they show up in the natural realm. God is a God that cannot lie. If He said it, then He will surely bring it to pass. We can't give up on the promises of God because they will surely come to pass in our lives.

Remember, God knew us before we were formed in our mother's womb, and He already has plans for our lives. He knows all the things that we would try before we discover who He has destined us to be in Him. When we are walking in unbelief, it is a major problem with us getting anything from God because faith is the currency

cessed 09-28-2019

of the Kingdom. Faith is what is going to get things moving to you in your life, but we must exercise our faith muscles and not give up even if we have some failures. You need to refuse to give up and keep pressing forward. It doesn't matter what it looks like now. You must know that everything will get better in your life, but you must grab the grace of God and continue to move from the sideline into the race. Because if you are running in the race with God, you already know that you are a winner!! And just know that we are walking from victory not walking to victory in Christ Jesus. We are victorious in Christ, Jesus!!

DECLARATIONS

If any of you lacks wisdom, you should ask God, who gives generously to all without finding fault, and it will be given unto you. (James 1:5 NIV)

But when you ask, you must believe and not doubt, because the one who doubts is like a wave of the sea, blown and tossed by the wind. (James 1:6 NIV)

That person should not expect to receive anything from the Lord. (James 1:7 NIV)

Such a person is double-minded and unstable in all they do. (James 1:8 NIV)

Trust in the Lord with all your heart, and do not lean on your own understanding. (Proverbs 3:5 ESV)

Be not wise in your own eyes; fear the Lord, and turn away from evil. It will be healing to your flesh and refreshment to your bones. (Proverbs 3:7-8 ESV)

Jesus immediately reached out his hand and took hold of him, saying to him, "O you of little faith, why did you doubt? (Matthew 14:31 ESV)

Because they did not believe in God and did not trust His salvation. (Psalm 78:22 NKJV)

Then they despised the pleasant land. They did not believe in His word. (Psalm 106:24 NKJV)

Yet with respect for the promise of God, he did not waver in unbelief but grew strong in faith, giving glory to God. (Romans 4:20 NASB)

However, they did not all heed the good news, for Isaiah says, "LORD WHO HAS BELIEVED OUR REPORT?" (Romans 10:16 NASB)

PRAYER

Father God, in the name of Jesus, I come before You today to ask that You help me to fully trust You and believe what Your Word declares about me in Jesus' name. Lord, I have a great need in my life. I feel the reason it seems like my prayers are not getting answered is that I am walking in doubt and unbelief. Lord, help me to believe that Your Word is true no matter what my circumstances say at this present moment. I cancel and veto the lies of Satan right now in Jesus' name. I will have what God said that I can have. Lord, I will read and study the Scriptures so that I will know what the promises of God are for my life. I cancel and veto all the lies that the enemy is telling me concerning my health, finances, marriage, and family right now in Jesus' name. Romans 10:17 (NKJV) says, "So then faith comes by hearing, and hearing by the word of God." So, I will continue to speak the Word back to You in prayer and declarations until what I am speaking manifests in the natural realm. Lord, if I should run into something in my life that is stubborn and won't let go of me, then I will fast and pray for the oppression to be removed out of my life in Jesus' name. Matthew 17:21 (NKJV) says, "However this kind does not go out except by prayer and fasting." I will continue to fast until anything that doesn't line up with the Word of God will be removed out of my life, so I can walk in the freedom that God provides for me. Lord, I thank You for Your love. You want to see me healthy, well, and living the abundant life in Your Kingdom in Jesus' name. Amen.

CHAPTER NINETEEN

Communion

Communion is defined as a Christian sacrament in which bread and wine are consumed as a memorial of a spiritual union between Christ and the body and blood of Christ, or intimate fellowship with Christ.[51] The Greek word for communion is "koinonia," which means partnership and spiritual fellowship.[52] Joseph Prince's article about "The Power of Holy Communion," states that Holy Communion is also known as the Lord's

51. "Communion" Merriam-Webster 2019 https://www.Merriam-Webster.com accessed 09-28-2019
52. Greek word for Communion "koinonia" https://www.biblehub.com accessed 09-28-2019

supper and represents the greatest expression of God's love for His people. Two items are used in Holy Communion-- the bread which represents Jesus' body that was scourged and broken before and during the crucifixion, and the cup which represents His shed blood. When Jesus walked this earth, He was never sick. At the cross, God took all our sicknesses and diseases and put them on Jesus' originally perfect and healthy body, so that we can walk with divine health. That is why the Bible says by His stripes, we are healed (Isaiah 53:5).

In Luke 22:20, Jesus tells us that the cup is the "new covenant in My blood." Apostle Paul tells us that the blood of Jesus brings forgiveness of sins. Besides being born again in Christ, a healthy body and mind are the greatest blessing anyone can have. Holy Communion is God's ordained channel of healing and wholeness. Today when we partake of the bread, we are declaring that Jesus' health and divine life flows in our mortal bodies. When we drink of the cup, we are declaring that we are forgiven and have been made righteous by Jesus' sacrifice. Jesus' blood gives us right standing before God, and we can come boldly into God's presence. When we pray, we can be sure that God hears us.[53]

I have been taking communion since November 2018 and I have noticed a change in my body. I am already off all the prescription medicines that I was taking. I used to be on Neurontin for nerve pain. I was on them for over three years but was able to wean off them. I was on Ambien for insomnia for three years also. I have been able to get off them as well in December 2018. I sleep very soundly every night. The last medicine that I wanted to get off was a hormone medicine called Estradiol. Beginning September 1, 2019, I am no longer on that medicine either. The only thing that I take is two vitamins twice a day and all is well. I contribute being able to get off all the medicines to taking communion every day and communing with God daily. I go into worship when He prompts me too because by His stripes I am healed. By His stripes cancer is healed. By His stripes blood pressures are normal. By His stripes Lupus is healed. By His stripes, the list goes to whatever you need Him to do in your body.

53. "The Power of the Holy Communion" by Joseph Prince
https://www.JosephPrince.org accessed 09-28-2019

The Communion table is the healing table. In an article by Kenneth Copeland talks about "Tips on How to Take Communion." He states that the communion table is for healing, deliverance, and confession. It's the powerhouse of God! Every time we take communion, it drives our roots even deeper into our faith in what the covenant of God means to us, and what the body and blood of Jesus has paid for us. We use our faith to take communion. We do so with determined purpose.[54] You don't have to wait until you are in church to take communion. You can take it at any time in your own home as often as you like. If I am down or feeling low or weary, I will go into worship and afterward, I am refreshed and strengthened. He also talks to me and tells me things that I write down on paper. I thank God for His presence because without it, I wouldn't make it. Psalms 91:1 (NIV) says, "Whoever dwells in the shelter of the Most High will rest in the shadow of the Almighty." When we are in the secret place with God, we can rest assured that we are protected from the storms of life.

54. "article, "Tips for Communion Healing by Kenneth Copeland https://www.kcm.org accessed 10-01-2019

DECLARATIONS

But he was pierced for our transgressions. He was crushed for our iniquities; the punishment that brought us peace was on him, and by his wounds we are healed. (Isaiah 53:5 NIV)

For the bread of God is the bread that comes down from heaven and gives life to the world. (John 6:33 NIV)

Then Jesus declared, "I am the bread of life. Whoever comes to me will never go hungry, and whoever believes in me will never be thirsty. (John 6:35 NIV)

For Christ also suffered once for sins, the righteous for the unrighteous, to bring you to God. (1 Peter 3:18 NIV)

He was put to death in the body but made alive in the Spirit. (1 Peter 3:18 NIV)

When he was at the table with them, he took bread, gave thanks, broke it, and began to give it to them. (Luke 24:30 NIV)

And he took bread, gave thanks, and broke it, and gave it to them saying, "This is my body given for you; do this in remembrance of me." (Luke 22:19 NIV)

In the same way, after the supper he took the cup saying, "This cup is the new covenant in my blood, which is poured out for you. (Luke 22:20 NIV)

Jesus said to them, "Very truly I tell you, unless you eat the flesh of the Son of Man and drink his blood, you have no life in you. (John 6:53 NIV)

Whoever eats my flesh and drinks my blood has eternal life, and I will raise them up at the last day. (John 6:54 NIV)

PRAYERS FOR COMMUNION BY PASTOR KENNETH COPELAND

Before you partake of the bread:

Lord, it's not right that I suffer from sicknesses or disease. I judge it now as being from Satan, and I reject it. I refuse to receive it any longer. I partake of the sacrifice of Your Son's body and I receive the abundant life that You have provided in Jesus' name. Amen.

Before you take the cup:

Father, I give You thanks for all You have provided for me through the New Covenant in Christ Jesus. I partake of those promises now! I am healed. I am redeemed. I am the head and not the tail. I am above and not beneath. I take the healing You sacrificed to give me, and I thank You and praise You for it, in Jesus' name. Amen. [55]

Another Prayer by Joseph Prince

Video on Youtube The Power of Communion

The body of our Lord, He said that my flesh is meat in it and my drink is drink in it.

Before you take the bread:

Lift it up before the Lord and say, "Lord Jesus by your stripes I am healed, make everything weak

---

55. Communion prayer by Kenneth Copeland https://www.kcm. org 10-01-2019

whole. My youth and strength are renewed like the eagles. My body is restored to that of a young man/young woman. By your stripes, through your grace, I will live to be 120 years old. My eyes will not be dim, my strength not abated, and the mind of a genius. Completely strong and healthy. Eat bread. We trust that healing is taking place. In the name of the Lord, Jesus let healing be in that body right now in the name of Jesus!!

Before you take the cup:

The blood has been shed, giving you regardless of how much you think that you have sinned against God. The blood that has been shed; God has a righteous foundation to heal your body. Amen, God wants you well. The righteous foundation is this, Jesus took the cup and said that this is the blood of the new covenant, for the forgiveness of sin, the sending away, the remissions of sins. In other words, when you drink this cup, you must not drink consciously of your sins still in your body, but you must drink in consciousness that it has been sent away. Like the scapegoat carries away your sin. Christ has taken away your sins. Drink. Amen.[56]

56.   Communion Prayer by Joseph Prince, Youtube video

SALVATION PRAYER

Father God, in the name of Jesus, I come before You today to ask that You forgive me for every sin that I have committed, knowingly and unknowingly, in thought and deed, omission and commission right now in Jesus' name. Lord, I know that I am a sinner, but I am asking for Your total forgiveness. Romans 10:9 says, "That if I confess with my mouth that Jesus is Lord and believe in my heart that God raised Jesus from the dead that I will be saved." I believe that Jesus died on the cross but rose again on the third day with all power in the palm of His hand. Lord, thank You for saving me and coming to live in my heart. Lord, I surrender my life and will for Your will in Jesus' name. Lord, send your Holy Ghost power to live in my spirit so I can be filled with Your power and Your fire in Jesus' name. Lord, thank You for making a new creature out of me. Old things have passed away and behold all things are new in my life in Jesus' name. Lord, I give You permission to remove anything that is in me and in my life that is not of You, Jesus. Thank You for Your unfailing love and Your grace and mercy in Jesus' name. Amen.

7 TYPES OF PRAYER

Communion: (All day / all the time)

Supplication: (Lifting up your Needs)

Intercession: (On Behalf of Others)

Spiritual Warfare: There are two types :

1. Dealing with yourself (Your Mind is the Battlefield), (Repentance and Forgiveness)

2. Dealing with Satan and demons (Putting on the Full Armor), (Binding & Loosing)

Prayers of Agreement (Corporate Prayer)

Watch & Pray (Continual State of Awareness as a Watchman on the Wall)

Prayers of Thanksgiving (Count your Blessings and Name Them One by One).[57]57

When we are praying, we are praying either one of more of these types of prayers. The word of God states that the "Effectual prayers of the

---

57. article "Seven Types of Prayer" by Rosalind Y. Tompkins
https://www.tallahassee.com accessed 10-03-2019

righteous availeth much and produce wonderful results." Even when it seems like we are praying, and nothing is changing, we cannot give up but continue to pray earnest prayers to Him. When we are in God's perfect timing for our lives, that is when things start to manifest. Many times, God is perfecting or growing us up in Him before He gives us something, so it doesn't destroy us. God wants to develop our character, integrity, and grow us up to full maturity before he releases some blessings in our lives. He must teach us to be good stewards over our finances, so we won't spend everything that we make. So, He can trust us with more money or financial blessings because He knows that You will give Your tithes and offerings faithfully regardless of the amount.

When it seems like we keep going around the same mountain repeatedly, it is because we have failed to learn the lesson that He is trying to teach us. Or it could be that He must set people in certain places or spots because He knows what you are going to need to bring the vision to pass in your life. We just have to be patient and keep on praying and believing that any day now, God will show up and show out in our lives like never before. It may seem impossible with you, but with God, He shows His power and glory the most when you have come to the end of yourself efforts. God can do a miracle like no other person can because He is the great creator and He can do anything but fail. So continue to lean and trust that God will do exactly what He has said and has planned for your life; even when you were just formed in your mother's womb, He already knew who you would be in His Kingdom and what you would be doing to advance His Kingdom in the earth.

CONCLUSION PRAYER
(GENERAL PRAYER)

Father God, in the name of Jesus, I come before You today to lift up everyone that will read or pray this prayer right now in Jesus' name. Lord, You said in Your Word that if two or three are touching and agreeing that You would be in the midst of them. Lord, I believe that You are in this prayer and that You hear me. Lord, I ask that You touch the hearts and minds of everyone who will read this book in Jesus' name. Lord, supply their every need such as Your riches in glory by Christ

Jesus. Lord, if they need finances, supply them. I call forth funds from the north, south, east, and west to hit their lives right now in Jesus' name. If they need healing in their bodies, Lord heal them because You said in Your Word that by Your stripes, we are healed in Jesus' name. Lord, let Your healing virtue saturate their hearts, minds, and bodies in Jesus' name. Lord, I command every stronghold that is plaguing their lives to be rendered null and void in Jesus' name. I command it to break and go back to the abyss from where it came from. Lord, I pray for lost loved ones.

Lord, send seasoned laborers in the paths of the family members that need salvation in Jesus' name. I pray that they will surrender their lives to Christ and stop running from Him. Lord, I pray for marriages. Lord, strengthen every marriage and let Your love flow through them and repair what needs to be repaired in them. Let both draw closer to You as they draw closer to each other in Jesus' name. Lord, I pray for all the single people who are reading this prayer in Jesus' name. Lord, let them pray to you concerning their spouses. Lead and guide them. Let them know that they are never alone in their walk with

You. Lord, give them supernatural strength so they would be able to wait for the spouses that you have picked out for them. We cancel and veto the spirit of loneliness right now in Jesus' name. I loose contentment to all the single men and women who are reading this prayer right now in Jesus' name. Lord, help them to feel loved and cherished by You in Jesus' name. Lord, heal every wounded and broken heart right now in Jesus' name. Psalm 147:3 (NIV) says, "He heals the broken hearted and binds up their wounds." Lord, we ask that You would take all the pain away from their hearts right now in Jesus' name. Lord, we thank You in advance for all that You have done for us up until this present time in Jesus' name. Lord, we give You all the glory, honor, and praise for being a loving God in Jesus' name. Amen.

References

1.   "prayer" Merriam-Webster.com 2019, https://www.Merriam-Webster.com   accessed 09-23-20191

2.   Greek word for prayer "proseuchoamia" https://www.biblehub.com accessed 09-23-2019

3.   "healing" Merriam-Webster 2019, https://www.Merriam-Webster.com   accessed 09-23-2019

4.   Greek word for healing "iama" https:// www.biblehub.com accessed 09-23-2019

5.   Mayoclinic.org, mental illness https:// www. mayoclinic.org accessed 09-23-2019

6.   "lunatic" Merriam-Webster 2019, https://www.Merrian-Webster.com accessed 09-23-2019

7.   Greek word for lunatic "seleniazetai" https://www.biblehub.com accessed 09-23-2019

8.   www.get-bible.com mental illness article accessed 09-23-2019

9. "forgiveness" Merriam-Webster.com 2019, https://www.Merriam-Webster.com accessed 09-23-2019

10.   Greek word for forgiveness "aphiemi" https://www.biblehub.com accessed 09-23-2019

11.   "patience" Merriam-Webster 2019, https://www.Merriam-Webste.com accessed 09-23-2019

12.   Greek word for patience "hupomone" https://www.biblehub.com accessed 09-23-2019

13.   "fear" Merriam-Webster 2019, https://www.Merriam-Webster.com accessed 09-23-2019

14.   Greek word for fear "phobos" https://www.biblehub.com accessed 09-23-2019

15. "Generational curses" Merriam-Webster 2019, https://www.Merriam-Webster.com accessed 09-23-2019

16.   Greek word for curses "katara" https://www.biblehub.com accessed 09-23-2019

17.   "carnality" Merriam-Webster 2019, https://www.Merriam-Webster.com accessed 09-23-2019

18.   Greek word for carnality "sarkikos" https://www.biblehub.com accessed 09-23-2019

19.   "confusion" Merriam-Webster 2019, https://www.Merriam-Webster.com accessed 09-24-2-19

20.   Greek word for confusion "akatastasia" https://www.biblehub.com accessed 09-24-2019

21.   "self-sabotage" Merriam-Webster 2019, https://www.Merriam-Webster.com accessed 09-24-2019

22.   Greek word for self-sabotage "sampotaz" https://www.biblehib.com accessed 09-24-2019

23. "40-day Soul Fast by Rebecca L. King 2015

24.   "anger" Merriam-Webster 2019, https://www.Merriam-Webster.com accessed 09-24-2019

25.   Greek word for anger "orge" https://www.biblehub.com accessed 09-24-2019

26. Journal behavioral Science & Law Statistics on anger accessed 09-24-2019

27. "It Cost Me Everything "Anger" by Prophetess Kimberly Moses and Co-Authors March 2019 accessed 09-24-2019.

28. "addiction" Merriam-Webster 2019, https://www.Merriam-Webster.com accessed 09-24-2019

29. Greek word for addiction "prosecho" https://www.biblehub.com accessed 09-24-2019

30. "depression" Merriam-Webster 2019, https://www.Merriam-Webster.com accessed 09-24-2019

31. Greek word for depression "tapeinosis" hhttps://www.biblehub.com accessed 09-24-2019

32. www.ask-angels.com, statistics for depression https://www.ask-angels.com accessed 09-25-2019

33. "Walking In Total Freedom After Healing From Deep Inner Wounds" by LaRose Angela Richardson accessed 09-25-2019.

34. "faith" Merriam-Webster 2019 https://www.Merriam-Webster.com accessed 09-25-2019

35. Greek word for faith "pistis" https://www.biblehub.com accessed 09-25-2019

36.   "lying" Merriam-Webster 2019 https://www.Merriam-Webster accessed 09-25-2019

37.   Greek word for lying "pseudomai" https://www.biblehub.com accessed 09-25-2019

38.   "lust" Merriam-Webster 2019 https://www.Merriam-Webster accessed 09-25-2019

39.   Greek word for lust "epithumia" https://www.biblehub.com accessed 09-25-2019

40.   "ungodly soul ties" Merriam-Webster 2019   https://www.Merriam-Webster.com   accessed 09-25-2019

41.   Greek word for soul "psyche" https://www.biblehub.com accessed 09-25-2019

42.   "ties"   Merriam-Webster   2019 https://www.Merriam-Webster.com   accessed 09-25-2019

43.   Greek word for ties "deo" https://www.biblehub.com accessed 09-25-2019

44.   article "Ungodly Soul Ties by Terri Savelle accessed 09-28-2019

45.   "witchcraft" Merriam-Webster 2019 https://www.Merriam-Webster.com   accessed 09-28-2019

46.   Greek word for witchcraft "pharmakeia" https://www.biblehub.com accessed 09-28-2019

47. "Unbelief/Doubt" Unbelief Merriam-Webster 2019 https://www.Merriam-Webster.com accessed 09-28-2019

48. Greek word for unbelief "apistia" https://www.biblehib.com accessed 09-28-2019'

49. "doubt" Merriam Webster 2019 https://www.Merriam-Webster.com   accessed 09-28-2019

50. Greek word for doubt" distazo" https://www.biblehub.com accessed 09-28-2019

51. "Communion" Merriam-Webster 2019 https://www.Merriam-Webster.com   accessed 09-28-2019

52. Greek word for Communion "koinonia" https://www.biblehub.com accessed 09-28-2019

53. "The Power of the Holy Communion" by Joseph Prince https://www.JosephPrince.org accessed 09-28-2019

54. "article, "Tips for Communion Healing by Kenneth Copeland https://www.kcm.org accessed 10-01-2019

55. Communion prayer by Kenneth Copeland https://www.kcm.org 10-01-2019

56. Communion Prayer by Joseph Prince, Youtube video www.JosephPrince.org accessed 10-01-2019

57. article "Seven Types of Prayer" by Rosalind Y. Tompkins https://www.tallahassee.com accessed 10-03-2019

About the Author

La Rose Angela Richardson is the wife of Richard Richardson and the mother of Satara Cowan. She has one granddaughter, Allara Cowan. She has lived in the Southeast Georgia area all her life. LaRose has worked in the nursing field for a total of twenty-two years. First, as a C.N.A for eight years, then going further in her studies in Practical Nursing. She graduated from Southeastern Technical Institute in June 1997 with a degree in Practical Nursing. She worked at a local nursing home in Vidalia, GA, for 14 years as an L.P.N. In 2009, she married Richard Richardson and moved to the city of Alma, GA, where they resided for nine years.

LaRose and her husband moved to Baxley, GA, in June 2018, where they live now. She is one of the co-authors of "It Cost Me Everything," which was written with Prophetess Kimberly Moses. Presently, LaRose attends Prophetess Kimberly Moses's Prayer line that meets Monday through Friday at 6 am and 12 pm. She is the author of "Walking In Total Freedom after Healing From Deep Inner Wounds."

She went to Crossland Christian University's Alma campus. Later she graduated with a Master's of Arts Degree in Theology on March 30, 2015, in Orlando, FL. She was ordained on May 29, 2015, at an ordination service before graduation at Crossland University.

She is a poetry writer with several poems published in "Our Great Modern Poets." She continued to pursue her education and later graduated with a Doctor's degree in Theology from Crossland University. She joined the Prayer line "Tongues of Fire" in November 2018 with Prophetess Kimberly Moses. She has been greatly empowered by praying in tongues for an hour each day Monday through Friday. Every wound or set back that she has gone through in her life has been for a purpose that was far greater than she could ever understand. All the troubles and trials were just a push to her so she could walk into her God-given destiny.

Index

A

B

R

Ingram Content Group UK Ltd.
Milton Keynes UK
UKHW021259200423
420496UK00022B/907